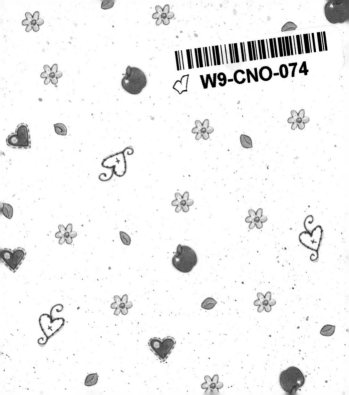

Thank you
Dear Teacher™

for:

Mrs. Wolfson

from:

Becky Wallin

date:

12-25-05

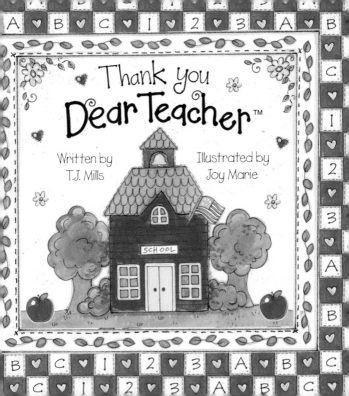

Thank you
Dear Teacher™

Written by
T.J. Mills

Illustrated by
Joy Marie

SCHOOL

Little Treasures Miniature Books

15 Things to Do With a Friend
15 Ways to Be Good to Yourself
15 Ways to Calm Your Soul
15 Ways to Spoil Your Grandchild
A Little Book of Blessing
A Roof With a View
Baby's First Little Book
Baby Love
Baby Oh Baby
Catch of the Day
Dear Teacher
For My Secret Pal

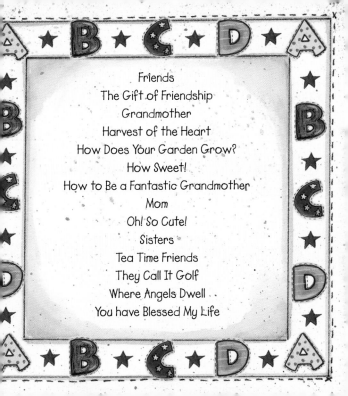

Friends

The Gift of Friendship

Grandmother

Harvest of the Heart

How Does Your Garden Grow?

How Sweet!

How to Be a Fantastic Grandmother

Mom

Oh! So Cute!

Sisters

Tea Time Friends

They Call It Golf

Where Angels Dwell

You have Blessed My Life

When a child succeeds
You reflect in the glow
But, dear teacher there are times
You may never even know –

That you:
Touched a heart,
Opened a door,
Created an interest
To learn even more.

That you:
Built self-esteem,
Brought courage around,
Inspired the dreams
Where a future was found.

For all these wondrous
Discoveries you've sparked,
We thank you dear teacher
From deep in our hearts.

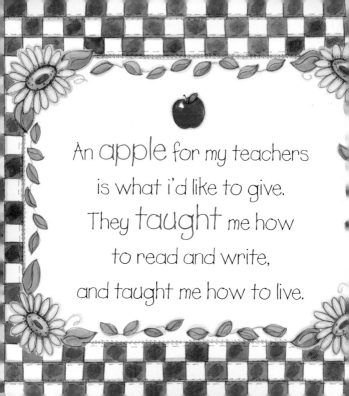

An apple for my teachers
is what i'd like to give.
They taught me how
to read and write,
and taught me how to live.

Of all the knowledge
We choose to borrow
A teacher's knowledge
Will brighten tomorrow

Blessed is the one who finds Wisdom.

PROVERBS 3:13

Teacher, trainer,
tutor, coach
Instill our children
with tomorrow's hope.
Professor, preacher,
schoolmaster, guide
Givers of knowledge
and holders of pride

A B C D E F G

All good

teachers start

with these!

The Book of KNOWLEDGE

LITTLE HOUSE

Once Upon a Time

Andrew Wyeth

Dictionary

The fruit of righteousness
will be Peace.

ISAIAH 32:17

A B C D E F

A TEACHER'S CREED

The present I can touch;

The future I can see.

The more that I give;

The more there will be.

1 2 3 4 5 6

ABCDEF
i ♡ learning
The Book of KNOWLEDGE
LITTLE HOUSE
Once Upon a Time
Andrew Wyeth
Dictionary
SCHOOL
Glue
1 2 3 4 5

The school year stands

before me now;

What will tomorrow bring?

It brings the song

that's in my heart

And the tune I choose to sing.

A TEACHER'S GARDEN

A teacher plants a garden
Every single year.
She tills it with a skillful hand
And waters it with cheer.

Each and every seedling
Is cared for in a way,
To give it every chance it needs
To blossom as it may.

Through rainy days and sunshine
The garden buds and grows;
The seedlings soak up all they can
Of what the teacher knows.

And when the growing season
Comes finally to an end,
The teacher
smiles so proudly
And prepares to
plant again.

If you laugh a lot, when you
get older your wrinkles
will be in the right place.

ANONYMOUS

The never was a person who
did anything worthwhile, who
did not receive more than he gave.

HENRY WARD BEECHER

★ Aim High. Think Big.
Every student can improve.

Believe in the student
even when he doesn't
believe in himself.

Care enough to correct,
to encourage, to challenge.

How does a
teacher do it?
We tried and tried
our best,
But our precious
little munchkin
Showed so little interest.

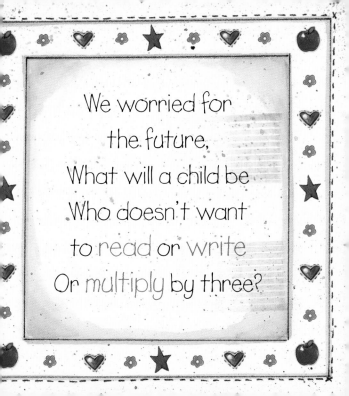

We worried for
the future,
What will a child be
Who doesn't want
to read or write
Or multiply by three?

So when the
"first day" came,
We hid our
parental fears
As the school bus
splashed on through
A puddle of our tears.

But, oh the
wondrous magic
We soon began to see;
Our doubtful little
offspring was on a
learning spree!

Our hearts were
filled with joy;
Sunshine filled the air.
The red stars on the
papers were the
answers to our prayer.

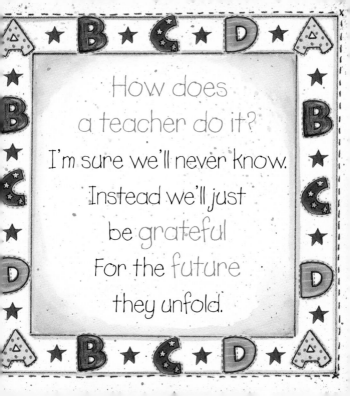

How does
a teacher do it?
I'm sure we'll never know.
Instead we'll just
be grateful
For the future
they unfold.

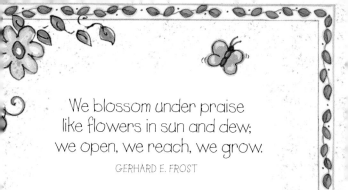

We blossom under praise
like flowers in sun and dew;
we open, we reach, we grow.

GERHARD E. FROST

Encourage one another
with these words.

I THESSALONIANS 4:18

My teacher is fond of history –
So I'm giving it a try.
My teacher is fond of questions –
So I've started to ask why.

Social Studies

Recess

Math

Biology

My teacher is fond of reading –
So I'm checking out more books.
My teacher is full of kindness –
So I've stopped the dirty looks.

My teacher is never tardy –
So I guess I won't be too.
My teacher likes to smile alot –
And that's why I'm smiling at you.

A
teacher,
like a master
gardener,
will make sure
that every sprout
gets its time
in the
sunshine.

DAILY INSPIRATIONS
FOR A TEACHER

The fruits of your effort
Will be sweet to taste.

Take a moment's pause,
For no reason than just – because.

Everyone should be quick to listen,
slow to speak
and slow to become angry.

JAMES 1:19

Dreams are the future
in rough draft!

There is time enough for
what we choose when
the time is rightly used.

To be happy and know it –
Is everything.

Happy people
leave a trail of Sunshine

Know your heart and
follow its path

Blessed is he who has found his work.

THOMAS CARLYLE

Education has for its object
the formation of character.

HERBERT SPENCER

It's what we learn after we
know it all that really counts.

ANONYMOUS

Education is the
best provision for old age.

ARISTOTLE

❀

Do everything in love.

I CORINTHIANS 16:14

❀

Where our work is, there let our joy be.

TERTULLIAN

Hope is the thing with feathers
That perches in the soul
And sings the tune without the words
And never stops – at all.

EMILY DICKINSON

Our deeds determine us,
As much as we
determine our deeds.

GEORGE ELIOT

He that would govern
others first should be the
master of himself

PHILIP MASSINGER

The wildest colts make the best horses.

ANCIENT PROVERB

Obedience and loyalty
Are learned through love.
What a child sees
Is what a child does.

Clothe yourself with compassion,
kindness, humility, gentleness
and patience.

COLOSSIANS 3:12

Tomorrow's
Efforts
Are
Created
Here

Respect

God,
family and country –
And the allegiance
to those we hold,
Are the patchwork of
grace and glory,
As each of our
lives are told.

The pledge of allegiance
is very important to me.
It helps me to think of
the people who died.
The pledge makes
me feel good.
It makes me think of God.
I am proud to say it.

HILLARY MILLS, AGE 8

I pledge allegiance to the flag of the United States of America, and to the republic for which it stands, one nation under God, indivisible, with liberty and j

America –

A country woven
by the notion
Of God, freedom
and devotion.